Limbo Stalking

Shaelyn Pagliaro

Presentation by *BookLeaf Publishing*

Web: www.bookleafpub.com

E-mail: info@bookleafpub.com

ISBN: 9789357440035

First edition 2023

DEDICATION

This is for my friends who love my unconditionally, my family who supports everything I do, and myself who kept pushing despite being knocked down almost every time.

ACKNOWLEDGEMENT

I am thankful for everyone who is and has been a part of my life. Everyone teaches us something if we only listen carefully enough.

PREFACE

"Those who dream by day are cognizant of many things which escape those who dream only at night."
- Edgar Allan Poe

Oblivious

Handsomely oblivious
Or maybe
Just biding time
Until we patiently dance into the start
Or, the dead oblivion that is our simple end
I am a moth where the darkness dreams
Come explore all that is beautiful about me
When I am open and most vulnerable
I dare you
Join me?

Space

I have always had my head up
Deep fascination with outer space
Maybe because I never belong
Or because I have always been told
Too much space is what I take
Physically
Metaphorically
Emotionally
I am too loud for most
I am not one that is missed
My absence is a relief
Felt by most

Solvable

I have always been a lover of puzzles
Of the solvable
Of the logical
And you are a mystery
I want to solve every night
You are euphoria to my aching soul
I want to feel your hands on my hips
As I rearrange the letters in your words
And create a new world for us to be in
Together

Body

A wound on the brain
I am a notorious skin picker
And this was just another scab
Omnivorous
Voracious
I pace
Yesterday was anxious
So is today
Everyday
Beautifully abundant but bitter
Blood on my tongue
A hungry screams
Plagues every intrusive thought
Seeps through every involuntary actions
Every motive

The absence of touch

Writing

5

Removing scars is always hard
Whether artist or animal
Creating life and worlds
Wielding the swords
That end a hero's tale
Throwing pebbles into the fountain
With every crossed-out word
Missing backspace key
Or worn-down eraser

Sandman

6

My slumber interrupted
By nightmares everlasting
Evil clutching
My bumpy burnt skin
Decaying
Delicate
Lost to wander
Never searching
Never finding
Walking
Pacing
Lost in a world
Crushed by the insects
Devoid of direction
Intoxicated by depression
Black as the deepest seas
Scorched through by words

Craving

I am a Monday at 2 p.m.
I mistake excitement for craving.
I am not graceful nor elegant.
If you could see my pain, you'd see scars and bruises.
I've grown numb to the full spectrum of human
emotions.
I'm waiting for a flame to re-ignite the embers in my
soul.
I crave you in the most innocent ways.
I crave your forehead kisses and be the hand you hold
at dusk.
It's your chest I want to rest my head on and your face
I want between my thighs.
I want to wake up next to you on Sunday mornings.
I want to watch movies and take pictures together.
I want to make love on sleepless nights and fuck you
till my legs shake.
I crave to be the one to tell you you're everything
when you feel like nothing.
I smoke too much and keep to myself a whole hell of a
lot.
I'm not unique. I am unexpected. I come on like the
storm brewing under my skin.

901

World dissolves and the weird parts start to
make sense
Thoughts race less and body calms from every
cell
Laughing, Smiling
Connecting the dots
Looking upon without being noticed
It's so simple
So perfectly calm
Peace and Security
Waiting for the taking

Dust

9

As I wish upon every star I see
I know they are only spheres of gases and rock
Everything is made up of space dust
and I remember my wishes are too

Killed

I killed her last night
Right there in my kitchen
It wasn't messy but it wasn't easy
It was peace taking hold
When I started to realize how alone I was
I knew I needed to kill those parts of me
That screamed my name while I slept
The parts of me that haunted everything I did
Everywhere I went
Everyone I met
I knew I had end it
So I killed her last night
It's not the first time
So my only thought was
"How long will it last now?"

Rebirth

A paradox in my own right
Wanting companionship without the drive for
eternity
I want to burn and conquer
Tear down everything in my way
I want to bathe in the ashes and decorate myself
with the charred pieces
Pieces of that old life
That old mind set
I want to drown in the tears of the past
Until I am reborn

Disintegration

I am a forlorn property of decay
A pit of screams and unsteadiness
Oppressiveness carved into my skin
Multivalent; different to each person
Contradicting myself at every left turn

Labyrinthian and Multilayered
I am a puzzle
I am a riddle
I am an enigma
But only to myself
I am open to no one that matters
Disassociating within myself
Falling into pieces by the hour
And putting myself back together every night

A Turing cypher
Like Cantor, infinite and unbounded
Just as complex as a Torquemada

High St

People drain me
Always have
Interpersonal interactions
Make me worn down,
Tired,
Ready for three days in the house
But, once in great while
I find someone who I am more empowered by
As opposed to drained of life
Someone I could spend an entire day with
And at the end,
I don't want to run away
I don't want to sleep for days
I don't want to hide
They put a face to security and calm
They feel like home

I have met very few people like this in my life
And you are now one of them
I may not do the same for you
You may not feel the same for me
But I know and I will always remember
How it was to feel secure and comfortable
In the presence of another human being

Demolition

I must say,
You're the only human being
That I currently know
That I don't get annoyed with
No matter how long we spend together
And for that,
I am grateful

I see no pain
No worry
Your face is a calm I aspire to
I wish to know how you
Conquer your demons
Rid of your desires
Rid of that addiction

And even if I am not the one you could love
Please don't clos yourself off from the
Possibility of loving someone
Building walls for protection can include
Unwanted moats
Unwanted perils
Where no one can get through
And when you wonder why no one sticks around
It may be too late
For demolition

Desire

15

As we mingle cravings
Feeding desires of the flesh
Knowing its something always wanted
A substitution
A secondary motive
A replenishment that leaves more desire
More interest
More time
More excitement that is mistaken as a craving
For desires of the flesh again

Resilient

I am tired of being called resilient, brave, strong
I want to be seen as soft, dafe, and comfort
I'm tired of not having a "me" in my life
I give and give and in the end
I'm just empty
I'm just alone
But I don't want to be hard
I don't want to be cold
I don't want to be distant
I want someone to fucking care
Maybe home is just a person you can be funny
with, care about, and hold once or twice a week
Home is abstract
Home is about safety and I've never felt safe
alone
Granted I love my solitude, but it can get old,
dusty
and the spiders only listen for so long
At this moment, I don't want to lay here alone
but I have no one
How do I not grow cold and distant while being
treated as such?
Mutual respect and care
That's all I am looking for

Random dance parties
Laughter
Cuddles on my small couch
Coffee or tea on cold nights
No commitment
No forever
No true love, soul mates, perfect relationship
bullshit
Love has never held anything together
I just need someone to lay here and rub my back
or play with my hair
until I fall asleep
Then, they can sneak away and when I wake up
I will feel better knowing they could at least stay
that long

Handsome

Hell will be beautiful baby
and flourish for you in the moonlight
our fears and dreams will blend until they obey
your smile is all that is needed

You

You have no idea
You don't see what is right in front of you every
fucking day
I am one hundred percent yours for the taking
We could watch this world burn brighter than the
fucking sun
and then I could rest my legs on your shoulders

Off

I can be anything you want me to be
You just have to tell me
It's more insulting to my intelligence than my
feelings f you don't just say
What you want and don't want
I don't know why communication is so hard
For everyone
I have opened the door so many times
And only felt the chill of winds
The iciness of a cold shoulder
Around here, the changing of the seasons
happen overnight
Turning it off
Setting Do Not Disturb on my life
Refocusing on what I want from myself
And myself alone

Bruises

You would think they would fall together with
bruised knees and an embrace strong enough to
put all their broken pieces back together
But it was the perfect pairing
So it was the wrong time

Music

To know her, deep down, is to know that she is
her music
In her soul, in her mind, in her heart
Just listen.
She is the darkest heavy metal and the sweetest
bluegrass
All at the same time
Always